HANDBOOK OF
FLORIDA FLOWERS

by

Lucille Procter

Illustrated by the Author

 PUBLISHING CO.
4747 TWENTY-EIGHTH STREET NO.
ST. PETERSBURG, FLA. 33714

ISBN: 0-8200-0405-7

REPRINTED: Dec. 1970; June 1971; Oct. 1971; Feb. 1972;
Jan. 1974; Sept. 1975; July 1976; Oct. 1977; April 1979;
May 1980; April 1981; July 1982

Manufactured in the United States of America

PREFACE

In presenting this book to the public we hope we have fulfilled a great need among flower lovers of the tropics and semi-tropics as well as the multitudes of visitors to Florida. The flowering plants illustrated here are the ones most likely to be seen in the gardens and therefore of the most interest. They include trees, shrubs, ground plants and vines.

There are three exceptions to the above which do not fall within the category of common garden plants. They are the two Orchids, Catleya (Faustia) and Phalaenopsis (Amabilis), and the Bird of Paradise or Strelitzia (Parvifolia). These need very special care, but to those truly dedicated to horticulture they provide great interest and do furnish a feeling of pride to the gardener.

It is sincerely hoped that this book will fulfill the need and furnish the interest desired by lovers of flowers in our land.

All material has been carefully checked with the works of Liberty Hyde Bailey, John Kunkel Small and Norman Taylor, authorities widely recognized in the field of botany.

POINSETTIA

Euphorbia (Pulcherrima)
Spurge Family

The Poinsettia, known as the Christmas Flower is a medium size shrub. It is a native of tropical America and blooms in the Winter. Although red is most popular there are also both pink and white varieties. It may be found growing in Florida, Mexico, Central America, the West Indies and the Bahamas.

The plant is propagated by cuttings taken in early Spring after the blooms are faded. In September several inches should be cut off the top of each stalk or branch. This will multiply the blooms at Christmas time. In Springtime the plants should be trimmed.

4

HIPPEASTRUM

Hippeastrum (Reginae)
Amaryllis Family

Although the blossom resembles that of the Lily, the Amaryllis family are tubers, whereas plants of the Lily family are bulbous . The color of the Hippeastrum is a rich, brilliant red fading to white in the center. It blooms from Spring to Fall and may be found in South Carolina, Georgia, Florida, Alabama, Louisiana, T e x a s, Mexico, Central America, northern South America, the West Indies and the Bahamas.

This is propagated either seed or separation. Seedlings will not bloom until the second year.

TURK'S CAP

Malvaviscus (Grandiflorus)
Mallow Family

A native of Mexico, this popular large shrub blooms all year. There are both red and pink varieties. The blossoms on this plant are unique in that they never appear to really open. It is used for hedges and screens. The Turks Cap may be found in Florida, Georgia, Alabama. Mississippi, Louisiana, Texas, California, Mexico, Central America, northern South America, the West Indies and the Bahamas.

This plant is propagated by cuttings and being very hardy will do well under almost any conditions and in any soil. It is very hardy and can withstand a considerable amount of frost.

HIBISCUS

Hibiscus (Rosa Sinensis)
Mallow Family

The Hibiscus, a native of Hawaii and China, blooms the year around. Two regional names are Shoe Black Plant and Chinese Rose. This variety is a brilliant red and is the most popular of many varieties and colors. In this hemisphere it will grow in Florida, southern California. Mexico, Central America, the West Indies and the Bahamas.

These flowers are grown mostly from cuttings. In full or partial sunshine they do very well. A moderate amount of water and annual fertilization should produce strong plants with beautiful blooms.

CROWN OF THORNS

Euphorbia (Splendens)

Spurge Family

The Crown of Thorns so aptly named is a native of Madagascar and in this hemisphere will grow in Florida. southern California, Mexico, Central America, northern South America, the West Indies and the Bahamas. It is a ground plant with a scarlet blossom and blooms in the Winter and Spring.

This plant thrives in any good garden soil as long as there is plenty of sun. They are propagated by seed or cuttings taken in the early Summer. Used as a border this spiny plant discourages intrusion. However they are best not used when there are little children nearby as their long stiff spines are very sharp.

BRAZILIAN PEPPER

Schinus (Terebinthifolius)

Cashew Family

This large shrub, which is a native of Brazil, has an insignificant blossom but the red berries hang in large bunches in the Winter. It is often called Christmas Berry or Florida Holly and is frequently used for Christmas wreathes and decorations. It is usually found in Florida, southern California, Mexico, Central America, northern South America, the West Indies and the Bahamas.

These plants grow in most any kind of soil and need little attention. However to insure their fruiting, both male and female trees must be planted as they are unisexual.

BOTTLE BRUSH

Calistemon (Linearis)
Myrtle Family

The long red stamens on this unique blossom certainly give rise to its name and beauty to its appearance even though the petals are small and unnoticed. It is a large shrub, native of Australia, and blooms most of the year. It will grow in Florida, southern California, Mexico, Central America, northern South America, the West Indies and the Bahamas.

Bottle Brush will grow in any soil but grows very slowly if there is much clay. Propagation can be by seed or cuttings. It will stand some frost.

MANDARIN HAT

Holmskioldia (Coccinea)
Verbena Family

We would have to go to the Himalayas to find this interesting vine in its native setting. Although it is not very well known in this hemisphere, to those who have one in their garden or have the good fortune to see them occasionally they are a source of delight. The blossom is red with a pale green saucer shaped calyx which is tinged with red around the edge. In this hemisphere it will grow in Florida, southern California, Mexico, Central America, northern South America, the West Indies and the Bahamas.

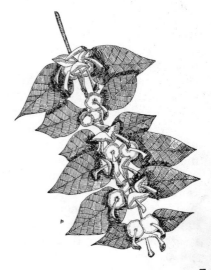

ROYAL POINCIANA
Delonix (Regia)
Pea Family

One of the most beautiful of flowering trees, the Royal Poinciana comes originally from Madagascar. Sometimes it is called Flame Tree or Peacock Flower because of its brilliant coloring. The blossom has four scarlet petals and the fifth one yellow, white and pink with red spots. It blooms in the Spring and Summer in the following parts of our hemisphere; Florida, southern California, Mexico, Central America, The West Indies and the Bahamas. This does well in most all soils in a well drained area and needs little attention.

The Royal Poinciana is a rapid growing tree and due to its wide spreading branches makes excellent shade.

POWDER PUFF
Calliandra (Haematoma)
Pea Family

This flower, like the Bottle Brush has long red stamens and an insignificant blossom, but forms a different shape, hence its name. A medium size shrub, native of tropical America, it blooms in Winter and may be found growing in Florida, Mexico, Central America, northern South America, the West Indies and the Bahamas.

Calliandra is propagated by seed. These should be soaked in warm water and left after it cools for a couple of days. Plant while the seeds are still wet.

There are also purple and white varieties. One hundred and twenty s p e c i e s are known.

KALANCHOE

Kalanchoe (Verticillata)
Orpine Family

This ground plant grows to about four feet high and has large clusters of bell shaped blossoms at the top. It is individual in its odd tubular shaped growth. The blossoms are bright red on the outside and somewhat paler on the inside. Kalanchoe originally came from South Africa. It blooms in the Winter and will grow in Florida, southern California, Mexico, Central America, northern South America, the West Indies and the Bahamas.

This Kalanchoe seems to do best from seed. It needs a well drained sandy soil and at least a half day of sun.

Some fertilization is necessary to give sturdy stalks.

FLAME OF THE WOODS

Ixora (Coccinea)
Madder Family

The blossoms of this interesting shrub are a brilliant scarlet and when in bloom they are so thick that the plant seems a mass of flame. It is a native of the East Indies and blooms in the Spring and Summer. In this hemisphere it will grow in Florida, southern California, Mexico, Central America, northern South America, the West Indies and the Bahamas.

Early Spring is the best time to take cuttings for propagation. Cuttings should have four pairs of leaves on each. If they are to be trimmed or shaped the best time to do this is after blooming is over.

9

TRANSVAAL DAISY

Gerberia (Jamesonii)

Composite Family

Blooms of this beautiful daisy are in all colors including pink, red, orange, salmon, violet and white. It is a native of Transvaal and blooms in the Spring and Summer. Another name for it is Barberton Daisy. It grows in many places in this hemisphere including South Carolina, Georgia, Florida, Alabama, Mississippi, Louisiana, T e x a s, Arizona, southern California, Mexico, Central America, northern South America, the West Indies and the Bahamas.

These are propagated best by seed and need a rich sandy soil mixed with peat.

DEVIL'S BACKBONE

Pedilanthus (Tithymaloides)

Spurge Family

A native of Tropical America, the Devil's Backbone is a ground plant which blooms in the Spring. Sometimes it is called Red Bird Flower or Slipper Flower, because of its color and shape. It may be found growing in Florida, Mexico, Central America, northern South America, the West Indies and the Bahamas.

A good sandy soil which is well drained is required by these succulent plants. They need plenty of sunshine also.

The Pedilanthus is similar to the Euphorbias in that they are succulents, and it would make an interesting addition to a flower bed given over to these.

SCARLET SAGE

Salvia (Splendens)
Mint Family

Scarlet Sage, a ground plant or small shrub, is a native of Brazil and is widely know throughout the United States but this particular variety is common to the warm climates. It may be found in South Carolina, Georgia, Florida, Alabama, Mississippi, Louisiana, Texas, Central America, northern South America, the West Indies and the Bahamas.

This plant is propagated by cuttings or seed. It does best in full sunlight but can be used elsewhere and still bloom fairly well. Too much water will retard the bloom.

COTONEASTER

Cotoneaster (Formosana)
Rose Family

The scarlet berries of this large shrub are what make it truly beautiful while its small white blossom is delicate and dainty. It is sometimes mistaken for Pyracantha which looks similar but has thorns which the Cotoneaster does not have. This is a native of Formosa and blooms in the Spring bearing fruit the following Winter, which is not edible. In this hemisphere it will grow in South Carolina, Georgia, Alabama, Mississippi, Louisiana, Texas, Arizona, California, Mexico, Central America, northern South America, the West Indies and the Bahamas.

MEXICAN FIRE VINE

Senecio (Confusus)

Composite Family

The fiery orange blossoms bring about the name of this native Mexican vine. It may be found blooming also in Florida, southern California, Central America, northern South America.

Mexican Fire Vine can be propagated by either cuttings or seed and also by division. It does well in any well drained rich sandy soil.

Although there are about 1,200 species o f Senecio growing throughout the world many are insignificant in appearance. Only about six are known and appreciated by flower lovers of this country. This particular variety makes a very showy addition to any garden and makes a delightful screen if grown on a fence or trellis.

DWARF POINCIANA

Poinciana (Pulcherima)

Pea Family

The Dwarf Poinciana is a medium size shrub which is native to the West Indies. The blossom is scarlet edged in yellow while another variety is all yellow. It blooms in the Spring, Summer and Fall, and may be found growing in Florida, southern California, Mexico, Central America, northern S o u t h America, the Bahamas as well as the West Indies.

This plant is propagated by seed which should be soaked in warm water for several hours to promote germination. It does well in most any soil.

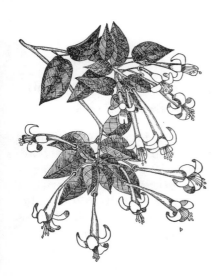

FLAME VINE

Pyrostegia (Ignea)
Bignonia Family

This beautiful vine with its bright orange blossom is one of the most showy plants of tropical America. It is a native of Brazil and blooms in the Winter. It may be found in Florida, southern California, Mexico, Central America, northern South America, the West Indies and the Bahamas.

A rich sandy soil with good drainage will keep Pyrostegia in good condition. Occasional fertilizing with well rotted cow manure is recommended. They are subject to mealy bug in some areas and should be sprayed once a week with a strong solution of kerosene and water.

BIRD OF PARADISE

Strelitzia (Parvifolia)
Banana Family

One of the most unique plants to be imported to tropical America, the Bird of Paradise is a native of South Africa. Petals are orange and the tongue is a deep, rich blue. The long bract is green edged in red, it blooms in the Winter and will grow in Florida, southern California, Mexico, Central America, the West Indies and the Bahamas.

The Strelitzia needs a rich soil and plenty of water and sunshine. Although the plant itself will stand neglect, it will not blossom under these conditions.

CAPE HONEYSUCKLE

Tecomaria (Capensis)
Bignonia Family

South Africa has sent us this beautiful vine with its hanging clusters of bright orange blossoms which come in the Spring and Fall.

This flower will grow in Florida, southern California Mexico, Central America, northern South America.

Cape Honeysuckle can be kept trimmed to shrub form, or if allowed to take its natural growth can make an excellent screen if grown on a trellis. With a good soil and average rainfall this does not need much attention.

Although there are several species native to tropical Amica, this African variety seems to be the only one commonly cultivated in Florida.

KALANCHOE

Kalanchoe (Fedtschenkoi)
Orpine Family

The Kalanchoe is a ground plant and is a native of Madagascar. This variety has a pale orange blossom with a light purple tint in the calyx and sometimes in the leaves. This flower blooms in the Spring and Summer; grows in Florida, south California, Mexico, Central America, northern South America, the West Indies and the Bahamas.

Kalanchoes sprout readily from seed or root from cuttings. They will do well in almost any moderate circumstance.

14

SILK OAK
Grevillea (Robusta)
Protea Family

The Silk Oak, though not really an oak, has somewhere along the line picked up the name. It originally came from Australia. The blossom is a beautiful feathery thing with long orange stamens while the petals are insignificant. Grevillea blooms in the Spring and will grow in Florida, Southern California, Mexico, Central America, northern South America, the West Indies and the Bahamas.

This beautiful tree can withstand drought to a considerable extent, and will endure some frost. Does well in either dense growth or open land. The seed is sometimes planted in pots as it makes a beautiful house plant while young.

GOLDEN DEWDROP
Duranta (Repens)
Verbena Family

The bright yellow berries on this large shrub hang in gorgeous bunches like Christmas tree ornaments in the Winter. The blossoms which appear in the Summer are about half an inch across and are a delicate lavender in color. It is a native of tropical America where another common name of Pigeon Berry, is bestowed. It may be found in Florida, southern California, Mexico, Central America, northern South America, the West Indies and the Bahamas.

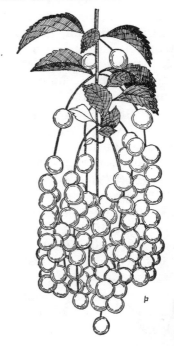

HONEY CUPS
Cassia (Bicapsularis)
Pea Family

Honey Cups is a shrub of considerable dimensions with beautiful yellow blossoms. It is a native of tropical America and may be found in Florida, southern California, Mexico, Central America, northern South America, West Indies and the Bahamas. The blooms appear in the Winter.

These flowers are propagated by cuttings and seeds. They love sunshine. A moderate amount of water is necessary, otherwise little attention is needed.

The leaves and pods of certain varieties of Cassia, sometimes known as Senna, are used for medicine. Others are used in tanning.

These often have vining tendencies and make an excellent screen.

YELLOW HIBISCUS
(Double)

Hibiscus (Abutiloides)
Mallow Family

One of the most beautiful of a beautiful family of flowers, the double yellow Hibiscus has been developed from a species found in the West Indies. A medium size shrub which blooms in the Spring and Summer, it may be found in Florida, the West Indies, northern South America and the Bahamas.

This Hibiscus seems to need special care for best results. A rich well drained soil, kept moist and fertilized in the Spring will be of advantage. Watering in the Winter is not necessary.

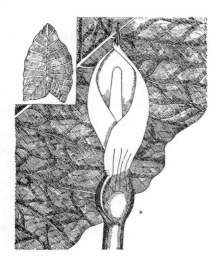

ELEPHANT EAR

Colocasia (Antiquorum)

Arum Family

The Elephant Ear with its huge leaves and large yellow blossom makes a showy addition to any garden. It is a ground plant which blooms in the Fall and is a native of tropical Asia. The Taro of Hawaii, from the roots of which the natives make poi, is another variety of the same plant. In this hemisphere it will grow in South Carolina, Georgia, Florida, Alabama, Mississippi, Louisiana, Texas, Arizona, California, Mexico, Central America, northern South America, the West Indies and the Bahamas.

Colocasia does best in damp, rich soil. Needs little attention if the right location is available.

ALLAMANDA

Allamanda (Cathartica)

Dogbane Family

This pretty yellow blossom grows on a vine which is native to South America. It blooms the year 'round and may be found in Florida, Central America, northern South America, the West Indies and the Bahamas. Children must be cautioned not to put them in their mouths as they are poisonous if taken internally.

It is easy to root cuttings of the Allamanda. This should be done in the Spring. It should be well watered during the Spring, Summer and Fall, but not in the Winter when the plant is partially dormant.

Used as a vine, it should be trimmed in the Spring, or frequent trimming as a shrub.

17

YELLOW OLEANDER
Thevetia (Nereifolia)

Dogbane Family

Another member of the Dogbane family, also poisonous if eaten, but an attractive medium size shrub. It is a native of tropical America and blooms most of the year, may be found growing in Florida, southern California, Mexico, Central America, northern South America, the West Indies and the Bahamas.

This plant yellow oleader needs a rich, sandy soil, somewhat moist, but not wet. It will tolerate some frost. Does well in either full or partial sunshine.

Sometimes this is called Trumpet Flower as are many other blooms of this form. Actually the name should not be used for any of them in order to avoid confusion.

YELLOW ELDER
Stenolobium (Stans)

Bignonia Family

This native tropical American plant is a large shrub, sometimes growing to tree size. Another name is Yellow Bells. It blooms in the Fall,and may be found growing in Florida, Georgia, Alabama, Mississippi, Louisiana, Texas, southern California, Mexico, Central America, northern South America, the West Indies and the Bahamas.

Propagated by seeds or cuttings, the Yellow Elder does Best in sandy and well drained soil. It is excellent to use as a screen, because of its dense growth. Some frost is tolerated. The seedlings will usually blossom at the end of the first year.

18

CATHEDRAL BELLS

Kalanchoe (Pinnatum)

Orpine Family

The podlike green calyx tinged in red is the most attractive part of this plant. The petals are red but mostly covered by the calyx. It is a ground plant and a native of tropical Asia. Another name for it is Air Plant, so called because it will grow without soil or water, deriving its moisture from the air. It blooms in the Winter and will grow in Florida.

Propagation by cuttings is simple but even a leaf dropped on the soil will take root and produce new growth quickly.

SPANISH BAYONET

Yucca (Aloifolia)

Lily Family

This strange plant sometimes grows to twenty-five feet in height but will bloom when quite small. The plant in this illustration was five feet tall and the blossom was reduced a great deal more than others in this book so as to show it to you in its entirety. It blooms in the Spring and is a native of tropical America. The Yucca may be found in North Carolina, South Carolina, Tennessee, G e o r g i a, Florida, Alabama, Mississippi, Mexico, the West Indies and the Bahamas.

Propagation of the Yucca is usually by seeds or offsets. Sometimes cuttings will do well. It needs a well drained sandy soil.

GOLDEN CHALICE

Solandra (Nitida)

Nightshade Family

This beautiful blossom is cream color with red veins. It grows on a large vine and is a native of Mexico. Golden Chalice blooms in the Winter in Florida, southern California, Mexico, Central America, northern South America, the West Indies and the Bahamas.

Golden Chalice likes plenty of sunshine. They grow best in a sandy soil and should be well watered throughout the Fall, Winter and Spring. Avoid fertilizing, as this tends to make more foliage and fewer blossoms.

The blossoms last four or five days and are from four to six inches long. These darken in color as they age.

CALADIUM

Caladium (Bicolor)

Arum Family

This ground plant is attractive all year around because of its colorful leaves which are green on the edge, turning to red towards the center with red veins. The pretty spathe-form blossom appears in the Summer and is cream color. There is also a variety with green and white leaves. The Caladium is a native of South America but may also be found in Florida, southern California, Mexico, Central America, the West Indies and the Bahamas.

Caladium is propagated by division of the tubers. In new plants the colors will not appear until the fifth or sixth leaf. This will do equally well in sun or shade but must be kept well watered.

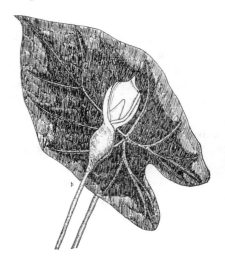

GARDENIA

Gardenia (Jasminoides)
Madder Family

One of the most fragrant of blossoms and one widely used for perfume is the Gardenia. Corsages from this pretty white flower are also in great demand. It grows readily in tropical America although it is a native of China. The bloom comes in Spring and Summer and it sometimes known as the Cape Jasmine. It can be found growing in Florida, southern California and Mexico.

The Gardenia is propagated from cuttings and should be planted in specially prepared soil which is four parts loam, one part sand and one part well rotted cow manure. The soil should be kept moist but not wet. The best position is in partial shade.

PERIWINKLE

Vinca (Rosea)
Dogbane Family

This attractive g r o u n d plant, seen profusely in Florida, is a native of Madagascar. Some blossoms are light rose with deep rose centers, some are white with deep rose centers and others plain white. The Periwinkle which is sometimes called Old Maid blooms all year. Besides Florida it will grow in Mexico, **Central America, northern South America, the West Indies and the Bahamas.**

This species of Periwinkle grows with little attention in sandy soil. It is an annual which continually reseeds itself. As the old plants die they can be removed.

MOSES IN THE BULRUSHES

Rhoeo (Discolor)

Spiderwort Family

Moses in the Bulrushes **is** a ground plant which is native to Mexico. Sometimes it **is** called Boat Lily or Oyster Plant. The upper sides of the leaves are green and **the** under sides are magenta. The boat-shaped bracts are magenta also, with tiny white blossoms growing from them. This interesting plant blooms all the year and may be found in Florida, Mexico, the West Indies and the Bahamas.

Plenty of moisture and partial shade is all that is required to grow sturdy plants.

There are only two known varieties. The other, vittata, has a yellow stripe on the leaves.

CHEROKEE ROSE

Rosa (Laevigata)

Rose Family

This lovely vine Rose has a beautiful white blossom. It is a native of China and blooms in the Spring and Fall. In this hemisphere it can be found growing in North Carolina, South Carolina, Georgia, Florida, Alabama, Mississippi, Louisiana, Texas, the West Indies and the Bahamas.

Cherokee Rose may be found growing wild in sandy well drained locations. Under these conditions it may be added to the garden with little or no care necessary.

SHRIMP PLANT
Beloperone (Guttata)
Acanthus Family

Rusty red bracts are the eye catcher on this unusual plant. It is a small shrub and is native of Mexico. The blossom is two petaled and white with a red pattern on the lower one. The Shrimp Plant blooms most of the year and may be found in Florida, southern California, Mexico, Central America, northern South America, the West Indies and the Bahamas.

Shrimp Plant will grow in any soil. It does best in partial sunlight with plenty of moisture.

Other varieties have red or purple blossoms. There are about 30 species in tropical America.

ANTHURIUM
Anthurium (Spathiphyllum)
Arum Family

The blossom of the Anthurium is a white spathe, graceful, tall and nodding. This is a ground plant and is a native of tropical America. It blooms in the Spring and may be found in Florida, Mexico, Central America, northern South America, the West Indies and the Bahamas.

Anthurium needs a humid atmosphere. A combination of moss, sand and rotted manure makes the best foundation. If roots appear above the surface they should at least be able to reach the soil.

CAMELLIA

Camellia (Japonica)

Tea Family

The Camellia is one of the most showy of flowers to be seen in the southern part of the United States and tropical America. It is a medium size shrub, native to China and Japan. The various colors are red, pink, rose, white and variegated.

The Camellia grows best in partial shade, in fairly damp places, however if well cared for they will do fairly well in drier soil with frequent watering.

The half double varieties are the easiest to care for as those with full double blossoms frequently drop their buds. They blossom in late Fall and early Winter.

SPIDER LILY

Hymenocallis (Keyensis)

Amaryllis Family

In Florida and the West Indies this graceful member of the Amaryllis family may be found in its natural setting. Although like a lily in appearance it is a tuberous plant rather than a bulbous one like the lily. It blooms in the Summer and is barely distinguishable from the variety known as Caymenensis which grows in the Bahamas. The Spider Lily is pure white.

Hymenocallis need no special care. Soil with peat is best, for good drainage. Propagation is by separation.

Plenty of sunshine is needed for good blooming although not necessarily all day.

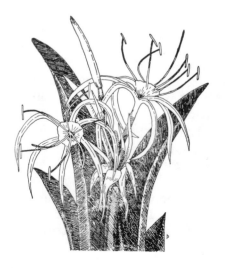

Golden Dewdrop

Sky Flower

Moses in the Bulrushes

Yellow Hibiscus (double)

Mexican F

Flame Vine

Hibiscus

Hippeastrum

Transvaal Daisy

Allamanda

gels Trumpet

Bird Of Paradise

Oleander

Cotton Rose

Crinum

Water Hyacinth

Rose Jasmine
Jasminum (Sambac)
Olive Family

STAR JASMINE
Jasminum (Nitidum)
Olive Family

CREPE JASMINE
Ervatamia (Coronaria)
Dogbane Family

Originally from India, these small shrubs have become a happy part of the gardens of tropical America. The Crepe Jasmine is not a real Jasmine but is commonly known as one. These all bloom in the Spring and Summer and will grow in Florida, southern California, Mexico, Central America, northern S o u t h America, the West Indies and the Bahamas.

These flowers are easily propagated from cuttings and do not need much care.

COTTON ROSE

Hibiscus (Mutabilis)
Mallow Family

This is especially interesting because while the blossom is white when fresh it turns dark red when it fades. The Cotton Rose, sometimes called Confederate Rose is a native of China and blooms in the Spring and Summer. It will grow in Florida, southern Louisiana, Mexico, Central America, northern South America, the West Indies and the Bahamas.

Cotton Rose does well in any light, well drained soil. Aside from watering through the dry spells and annual fertilizing it needs very little care.

PINEAPPLE GUAVA

Feijoa (Sellowiana)

Myrtle Family

One of the well known fruits of tropical America, the Pineapple Guava is ornamental as well as edible and has a white blossom with long red stamens. It is a small tree and a native of South America. The bloom comes in the Spring and the edible fruit in early Fall. Guava may be found growing in Florida, southern California, Mexico, Central America, northern South America and the West Indies.

This fruit grows best in a rich loam which is well drained. It will stand light frosts, but will not do well in excessive humidity. Feijoa will live through dry spells but needs plenty of water to produce good growth.

ANGELS TRUMPET
(Double)

Datura (arborea)
Nightshade Family

This small tree with the trumpet-like blossoms is a native of Peru and Chile. The blossoms of other varieties are red, yellow or violet. It is poisonous if taken internally. The blossoms of Datura (arborea) are white. They appear in Spring, Summer and Fall, and it may be found growing in Florida, southern California, Mexico, Central America, northern South America, the West Indies and the Bahamas.

These plants need plenty of root space and plenty of water, in a well drained soil. Beautiful blooms are obtained with very little trouble.

PLUMBAGO

Plumbago (Capensis)

Leadwort Family

Plumbago is a medium size shrub, or sometimes a vine, with a delicate pale blue blossom. It is a native of South Africa and may be found in Florida, southern California, Mexico, Central America, northern South America, the West Indies and the Bahamas. This flower blooms all of the year.

They grow well from cuttings, which, if taken in the Fall will bloom the following Summer. Plumbago needs full sunshine to produce blossoms of full color.

There is another variety, rosea, with a deep red blossom. The blooms of both of these resemble the phlox to some extent, particularly the latter.

BLUE SAGE

Eranthemum (Nervosum)

Acanthus Family

The blue sage is an unusually interesting plant with blue blossoms and white leaf shaped bracts with green ribs. It is a medium size shrub. A native of India, its blooms appear in the Winter and Spring. In this hemisphere it may be found growing in Florida, southern California, Mexico, Central America, northern South America, the West Indies and the Bahamas.

This plant needs rich sandy soil for best results. Should also be grown in well-drained soil.

It is prapogated by cuttings and needs plenty of sun and water.

27

LUPINE
Lupine (Diffusus)
Pea Family

Lupine, or Deer Cabbage as it is sometimes called, blooms in the Spring and Summer. Although this variety is limited to a small area in the southern part of the United States there are many other kinds growing in parts of the tropics and subtropics. You may find it in North Carolina, Florida, Alabama and Mississippi.

The Lupine can easily be grown in any soil providing it does not contain lime. They are propogated by division.

The flowers of this variety are blue, while others are yellow or white.

SKY FLOWER
Thunbergia (Grandiflora)
Acanthus Family

The Sky Flower is a vine which is native of India. The blossom is lavender and is seen in the Summer and Fall. Some varieties are blue and some are white. In this hemisphere it will grow in Florida, southern California, Mexico, Central America, northern South America, the West Indies and the Bahamas.

This flower is the hardiest and most common as well as the most beautiful of the Thunbergias. It can easily be propogated from cuttings and will blossom if plenty of space for growth is allowed.

AGERATUM
Ageratum (Conyzoides)
Composite Family

The Ageratum is a ground plant and is native of tropical America. This one is lavender but there are also white and blue varieties. It blooms in the Summer and Fall and may be found growing in Florida, southern California, Mexico, Central America, northern South America, the West Indies and the Bahamas.

These interesting plants will thrive in any soil and will sprout readily from seed.

They are excellent border plants and although the Ageratum is an annual, the seedlings can be reset when they sprout each Spring, to keep the border in line. It is an attractive blossom for bouquets.

JACARANDA
Jacaranda (Acutifolia)
Bignonia Family

One of the most beautiful trees of the tropics and semi-tropics, is the Jacaranda. It is just like a huge bouquet when in full bloom. The blossoms are lavender and the feathery leaves help give this illusion. It is a native of Brazil but may also be found growing in southern California, Mexico, Central America, northern South America, the West Indies and the Bahamas.

The Jacaranda may be propagated by cuttings. It needs a well drained soil and occasional fertilization.

There are about 50 species but only two are known in Florida.

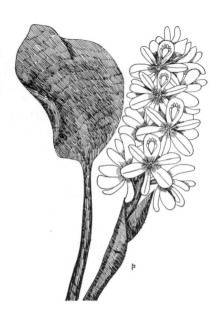

WATER HYACINTH

Eichhornia (Crassipes)

Pickerel Weed Family

The interesting part of this water plant is that one petal has a yellow spot with a blue pattern on an otherwise purple petal. The other petals are all purple.

Other names for this flower are River Raft and Wampee.

This scourge of the Florida waterways was imported from Japan by a woman who took a fancy to the delicate blossom.

The blooms come in the Summer and Fall, at which time rafts of the plant break loose and drift with the current on Florida rivers, often choking the river completely.

The state of Florida has spent many millions of dollars in eradication programs but the hardy water plant defies extinction.

VITEX

Vitex (Agnus-castus)

Verbena Family

Vitex is a small tree, a native of southern Europe. This plant is unique in the fact that the blossoms appear on the ground shoots as well as on the tree. It blooms in the Summer and Fall. In this hemisphere it will grow in North Carolina, South Carolina, Georgia, Florida, Alabama, Mississippi, Louisiana, Arkansas, Texas, New Mexico, Arizona, California. Mexico, Central America, northern South America, the West Indies and the Bahamas. The blossom is purple.

Vitex will grow in almost any soil that is well drained, and is in the open sun. It will grow easily from seed or from green cuttings.

KING'S MANTLE

Thunbergia (Erecta)
Acantha Family

The King's Mantle, some-
times known as Monarch's
Robe is a medium size shrub.
The blossom has a cream col-
or tube with purple petals.
There is also a white variety.
It blooms in the Spring and
is a native of tropical Africa.
In this hemisphere it will
grow in Florida, southern
California, Mexico, Central
America, northern South
America, the West Indies
and the Bahamas.

King's Mantle is started
either by seed or cuttings of
the new shoots, which can be
rooted. They usually do not
bloom until the second season.

BEAUTY BERRY

Callicarpa (Americana)
Verbena Family

Magenta berries bring this
medium size shrub to the full
power of its beauty in the
Summer and Winter. The
blossoms which are bluish in
color appear in the Spring
and Fall. Sometimes it is
called French Mulberry. It is
native to the southern United
States and may be found in
North Carolina, South Carolina, Georgia, Florida, Alabama, Mississippi, Louisiana,
Texas and Arkansas.

Beauty Berry can easily be
grown from seeds or cuttings.
If they die back from frost
new shoots come up readily.
It makes a beautiful hedge
when trimmed.

BOUGAINVILLEA

Bougainvillea (Glabra)

Four o' Clock Family

The showy part of this large shrub is the magenta bracts. Each of these contain three small yellow blossoms. It is sometimes called Paper Flower. There are two other common varieties which are vines. One is salmon color and the other is crimson. Bougainvillea is a native of South America and blooms most of the year. It may also be found in Florida, southern California, Mexico, Central America, northern South America, the West Indies and the Bahamas.

With plenty of sunshine the Bougainvillea will grow in most any soil and will root easily from cuttings.

RUBBER VINE

Cryptostegia (Grandiflora)

Milkweed Family

Usually a vine, but sometimes a shrub, Cryptostegia is a native of Africa. The blossoms are purple and so similar to Purple Allamanda that it is often mistaken for that flower. It blooms in the Summer and will grow in Florida, southern California, Mexico, Central America, northern South America, the West Indies and the Bahamas.

Cryptostegia does well in most ordinary garden soil. It is propagated by cuttings in the spring.

The juice when exposed to the sun produces pure India rubber—and is grown for this purpose.

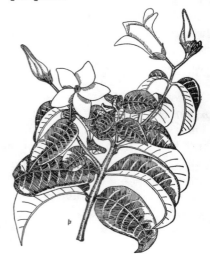

PANDOREA

Pandorea (Ricasoliana)

Bignonia Family

This vine is a native of South Africa. Has beautiful violet blossoms with red veins. Blooms in the Summer and will grow in South Carolina, Georgia, Florida, Alabama, Mississippi, Louisiana, Texas, Arizona, California, Mexico, C e n t r a l America, northern South America, the West Indies and the Bahamas.

Pandorea needs a rich soil and is grown best from seed. If parts are touched by frost these should be cut down at once and usually the plant can be saved. It needs full sun and it is four or five years before blooms appear.

ASSONIA

Dombeya (Nairobensis)

Sterculia Famiiy

Large heads of hanging clusters describe the beautiful pink blossoms of this large shrub from Madagascar. It blooms in the Winter and in this hemisphere will grow in Florida, southern California, Mexico, C e n t r a l America, the West Indies and the Bahamas.

This is a very showy shrub which needs very little attention and is one of many species.

With the advent of the airplane which brought us within easy reach of central Africa, many new species were discovered, bringing t h e i r kind to nearly 100 in number. Although the Dombeya is little known in this hemisphere it is well worth while to seek out and propagate.

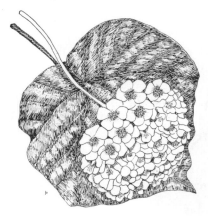

BEEFSTEAK BEGONIA
Begonia (Feastii)
Begonia Family

One of the lovliest of the Begonia Family, this ground plant is a hybrid of two native Mexican varieties (Manicata and Hydrocotylifolia). It is named Beefsteak Begonia because of the deep red of the underside of the leaf. The blossom is a pretty pink, which appears in the Winter.

May be found in Mexico, Florida, southern California, Central America, northern South America, the West Indies and the Bahamas.

This type of Begonia can be propagated by seed or leaf clipping. It must be protected from frost, sun and dryness.

Other varieties are found in many shades of rose, scarlet or yellow. Some are pure white.

CORAL VINE

Antignon (Leptopus)
Buckwheat Family

The Coral Vine is a native of tropical America and grows to cover a large area if there are either natural or built supports for it. It makes a beautiful cover of profuse pink blossoms, in the Spring, Summer and Fall. Other names for it are Mountain Rose, Pink Vine and Tallahassee Vine. It may be found growing in Florida.

The Coral Vine will die down when touched by frost, but new shoots will always come up in profuse growth the following Spring. New plants are always coming up from seeds which have dropped to the ground and these may easily be transplanted.

PENTAS

Pentas (Lanceolata)
Madder Family

The Pentas is a medium size shrub and is a native of Africa. There are other varieties in red, rose, lilac and white. This one is pink with red tubes. In this hemisphere it will grow in Florida, southern California, Mexico, Central America, the West Indies and the Bahamas.

Pentas need a well drained soil and plenty of water in Spring and Summer. They should be started in the shade but after well rooted, transfered to a sunny spot.

Cuttings of half matured wood will bring best results. Although only one specie is known in this hemisphere, there are about 30 in tropical Africa.

OLEANDER

Nerium (Oleander)
Dogbane Family

This is a large shrub, another one of the Dogbane family which is poisonous if taken internally. It blooms all of the year. This is a pink variety. Another is white. Oleander is a native of the Levants. Sometimes it is called Rose Bay. In this hemisphere it will grow in Florida, southern California, Mexico, Central America, northern South America, the West Indies and the Bahamas.

Oleanders are very hardy but in some areas need constant spraying to save them from being eaten by caterpillars. Grown in the open sunshine they will bloom profusely.

LANTANA

Lantana (Camara)

Verbena Family

Lantana is a small shrub and is native of the West Indies, Texas and Florida. The blossoms grow in small formal clusters in pink, orange or yellow. Sometimes all three colors appearing in the same cluster. There is also a purple variety. It blooms in the Spring. Besides in the above places it may also be found growing in South Carolina, Georgia, Alabama, Mississippi, Louisiana, New Mexico, Central America, northern South America and the Bahamas.

Lantana will grow in any soil but needs plenty of sun. After the plant is well started it can withstand long dry spells. Cuttings root easily.

AZALEA

Rhododendron (Reticulatem)

Heath Family

This small shrub came from Japan to grace the gardens of southern United States. This variety is rose-pink and blooms in the Spring. Other varieties are white, salmon, deep rose and dark red in varying sizes. They may be found in Virginia, North Carolina, South Carolina, Georgia, Florida, Alabama, Mississippi, Louisiana, Texas, Arkansas and Tennessee.

A mixture of peat and sandy soil is best for azaleas. They do best in partial shade. As the roots are near the surface, loosening of the soil should not be attempted.

Not much water is needed after they are well started.

CRAPE MYRTLE

Lagerstromia (Indica)
Looseestrife Family

Rose pink is the color of this variety of Crape Myrtle. It blooms in the Summer and Fall. There are also purple, white and red varieties. Another name is Ladies' Streamer. This is a large shrub and a native of Asia. In this hemisphere it will grow in North Carolina, Virginia, Georgia, Florida, Alabama, Mississippi, Louisiana, Texas, Arkansas, New Mexico, Arizona, California, Mexico, Central America, northern South America, the West Indies and the Bahamas.

The best method of propagation is with cuttings which will usually bloom the following season.

BAG FLOWER

Clerodendron (Thompsonae)
Verbena

This is a small shrub with vining tendencies. A native of West Africa. Another name is Glory Bower. It blooms in the Spring, Summer and Fall. This variety has a red flower with a white bract while there is another with a red bract. In this hemisphere it will grow in Florida, southern California, Mexico, Central America, Central America, northern South America, the West Indies and the Bahamas.

Clerodendron grows best in the shade and does not need much attention.

When it is kept trimmed it can make an excellent hedge.

CRINUM

Crinum (Zeylanicum)

Amaryllis Family

Crinum, like other members of the Amaryllis family has a lily-like blossom. It is a ground plant from tropical Asia, a welcome addition to the tropical gardens of this hemisphere. The blooms appear in Spring and Summer. The petals are red and white in stripes and has a deep red stem. This plant will grow in Florida, South Carolina, Georgia, Alabama, Mississippi, Louisiana, Texas, the West Indies and the Bahamas.

The small offsets of the roots can be detached to start new plants and these root very easily. Grown from seed it takes two or three years to bloom.

This is a rich and colorful addition to any garden.

MOUNTAIN EBONY

Bauhinia (Variegata)

Pea Family

The blossoms of this tree are so similar in appearance to Orchids that it is sometimes called Orchid Tree. It is a native of Indo-China and blooms in the Winter. This variety is deep red with some yellow coloring between the ribs on the lower petal. The other petals have fading color towards the center. There are also orchid color varieties as well as white. In this hemisphere it will grow in Florida, southern California, Mexico, Central America, northern South America, the West Indies and the Bahamas.

The Bauhinia needs well drained soil. It is easily grown from seed and fairly free of pests.

PHLOX

Phlox (Drummondii)

Polemonium Family

A native of Texas, this ground plant blooms in the Spring and Summer. This variety is deep red. There are others which are purple, pink or white. It may be found in Florida, Georgia, Alabama, Mississippi, Louisiana and of course Texas. There are other species which are widely grown throughout other parts of the United States.

Propagated from seeds, cuttings or root division they grow best in the open sunlight. Old plants should be cut back; the roots divided and the new growth will equal that of new plants. Rich soil and plenty of water will give best results.

CARDINAL'S FEATHER

Jacobinia (Coccinea)

Acanthus Family

The deep red Cardinal's Feather is a large shrub, and is a native of South America. It blooms in the Summer and may be found in South Carolina, Georgia, Florida, Alabama, Mississippi, Louisiana, Texas, New Mexico, Arizona, California, Mexico, Central America, northern South Ameicra, the West Indies and the Bahamas.

This plant needs plenty of water. It roots easily from cuttings.

After these have bloomed once, they become less attractive, so it is best to keep new plants coming along each Spring and dispose of the old ones.

NIGHT BLOOMING
CEREUS

Selenicereus (Grandiflora)

Cactus Family

This is a trailing or climbing Cactus with aerial roots. It has a gorgeous white blossom with yellow stamens which is a sight to behold on a moonlight night, as the older plants frequently have well over a hundred blossoms at a time. It is a native of Jamaica and Cuba and may also be found on other islands of the West Indies, the Bahamas, Central America, Mexico and Florida.

It is named for the moon goddess Cereus.

This does best in sandy soil and with no water other than the natural rainfall.

There are more than 20 species of Selenicereus. This one has some medicinal use as a heart stumulant.

PASSION FLOWER

Passiflora (Violacea)

Passion Flower Family

This variety of Passion Flower is lavender with a lavender and white crown. A native of Brazil, it grows on a vine and blooms in the Spring. It may be found growing in Florida, Mexico, Central America, northern South America, the West Indies and the Bahamas.

The Passion Flower is easily propagated by cuttings.

In some of the varieties the blossoms are yellow, green or red. A few of the Passiflora are grown for their edible fruit.

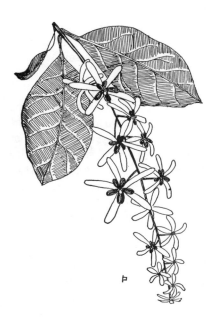

QUEEN'S WREATH

Petrea (Volubilis)

Verbena Family

The Queen's Wreath, sometimes called Purple Wreath is a vine which blooms in the Spring. Although it is a native of Mexico, Central America and the West Indies, it may also be found growing in Florida, northern South America and the Bahamas.

This may be propagated by cuttings in the Spring. It is very sensitive to frost and must be protected in regions where occasional frost appears.

The double blossom is unque. The smaller petals are rich purple and the larger lavender.

PRIVET

Ligustrum (Walkeri)

Olive Family

Various varieties of the Privet are known throughout the world for use as hedges. This particular one is a native of Ceylon and is widely used in tropical and semi-tropical America. It has a small white blossom which grows in stiff erect panicles on a medium-size shrub. The blossom appears in the Spring. The specific places where it may be found in this hemisphere are Florida, Mexico, Central America, the West Indies and the Bahamas.

The Privet can be grown from seed or cuttings can be rooted. The Privets are one of the hardiest of plants and will grow in most any soil and live under the most difficult of conditions.

PHALAENOPSIS

Phalaenopsis (Amabilis)

Orchid Family

The Phalaenopsis, some-
times known as the Moth Orchid, blooms in May or June.
It is a beautiful white color
with stains of deep yellow and
purple spots toward the center. It is a native of the May-
layan archipelago and will
grow out of doors in Key West
but can only be hot house
raised further north. Under
the right conditions it might
be grown outdoors in other
parts of the American tropics.
Its natural habitat is in rocks
and trees near water.

The growing of orchids is
very specialized. Persons in-
terested in the culture of these
air plants should consult
books written by specialists
that are obtainable in most
public libraries.

ORCHID

Catleya (Faustia)

Orchid Family

This is the best known of
the Orchids and the most
popular for corsages. Most
of the Catleyas supplied by
florists throughout the United
States are grown in hothouses
in Florida and California. In
southern Florida they can be
grown out of doors. This flower blooms the year around on
a plant which is twelve to
fourteen inches in height. It is
the familiar color from which
the well known "orchid col-
or" is derived. Outstanding
is the purple lip. Native to
Central America, South Brazil, Colombia and Venezuela,
grows at high altitudes in its
natural habitat, hence its di-
vergence of origin.

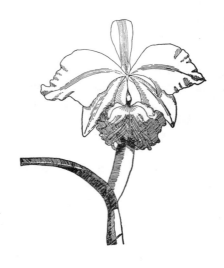

CLOCK VINE

Thunbergia (Affinis)
Acanthus Family

The Clock Vine is a shrub
with vining tendencies and
sometimes appears as one and
sometimes the other. The
blossom is a bluish - purple
with a yellow - white tube.
There is also a white variety.
It is a native of tropical Africa and in this hemisphere
may be found in Florida,
southern California, Mexico,
Central America, northern
South America, the West Indies and the Bahamas. Blooms
appear in the Spring and
Summer.

They can be propagated by
cuttings and grow very rapid-
ly. Severe pruning prevents
the blossoms from forming.

NATAL PLUM

Carissa (Grandiflora)
Dogbane Family

A medium-size shrub, the
Natal Plum is sometimes
called Amatungula. It has
white blossoms and soft spines
whereas some other varieties
have pink or purple blossoms
and have stiff spines. A native of South Africa, in this
hemisphere it may be found
in Florida, southern California, Mexico, Central America,
northern South America, the
West Indies and the Baha-
mas. Blooms in the Spring.

The Carissa is especially
r e c o m m e n d e d for hedge
plants.

GAILLARDIA

Gaillardia (Fistulosa)
Composite Family

GAILLARDIA

Gaillardia (Lanceolata)
Composite Family

The Gaillardia Fistulosa is yellow, while the Lanceolata is deep red, changing to yellow at the ends of the petals. It blooms in the Spring and Summer and is native to the southern United States.

Light open soil and plenty of sunshine are all these plants need to beautify your garden. Occasional use of commercial fertilizer will give improved blossoms.

The Gaillardia (lanceolata) may be seen growing wild throughout Florida, thus establishing its hardy nature.

CROSSANDRA

Crossandra
(Infundibuliformis)
Acanthus Family

The Crossandra is a small shrub and is especially interesting because of the unique blossom whose petals extend only about two-thirds of the way around its center. The color is orange. It is a native of India and in this hemisphere may be found in Florida, Mexico, Central America, northern South America, the West Indies and the Bahamas. It blooms in the Spring and Summer.

This plant needs a warm, moist greenhouse with a rich but sandy soil. Can be propagated by cuttings. Some species have red blossoms and others yellow.

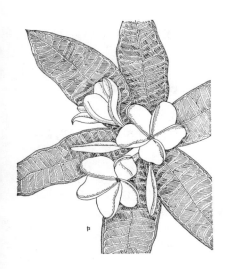

FRANGIPANI

Plumeria (Acutifolia)

Dogbane Family

The Frangipani is a beautiful tropical flower growing on a small tree. It is a native of the West Indies and may be found in Florida, Mexico, Central America, northern South America and the Bahamas. The blossoms are white with yellow centers which appear in the Spring and Summer.

There are about 50 species, all of tropical America. Blossoms of others are all white, all yellow or rose-purple. The Frangipani is one of the most fragrant of blossoms.

These can be propagated by cuttings in early Spring.

JERUSALEM THORN

Parkinsonia (Aculeata)

Pea Family

A lovely feathery plant with pretty yellow blossoms. This small tree or shrub is a native of the American tropics. It may be found in Florida, Mexico, Central America, northern South America, the West Indies and the Bahamas. It blooms in the Spring and Summer.

The Jerusalem Thorn can stand drought and frost to a remarkable degree for a tropical plant. It is only one of the many beautiful flowering trees of the Pea family. Another is the Poinciana.

There are five varieties of Parkinsonia but this is the most widely grown.

MAGNOLIA

Magnolia (Grandiflora)
Magnolia Family

This is a large tree some-times growing to eighty feet, with the most gorgeous large white blossoms. It has purple stamens. The blooms appear from May to August. This particular variety is a native of southeastern United States and may be found in North Carolina, S o u t h Carolina, Georgia, Florida, Alabama, Mississippi, Louisiana a n d Texas.

A well drained soil is more important than a rich soil for Magnolias. Well rotted cow or horse manure is best for fertilizing and should be used every two years. They do not withstand transplanting very well.

MORNING GLORY

Ipomaea (Mutabilis)
Morning Glory Family

This variety of Morning Glory is a native of tropical America. It is a vine which blooms in the Spring and Summer. The blossom is blu-ish purple with a white tube. Other varieties are magenta, red, rose, yellow, lilac, white and pink. This tropical va-riety may be found in Flor-ida, Mexico, Central Amer-ica, the West Indies and the Bahamas.

Morning Glories will grow in almost any soil. The seed is very hard and will sprout sooner if notched.

This tropical variety is a perennial and makes a nice permanent screen on a fence or trellis.

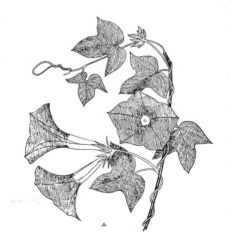

INDEX OF COMMON NAMES

INDEX OF LATIN NAMES